MELINDA PARKHURST

Stories of Myself

Your journey of self-discovery through storytelling, mindfulness, movement, and creativity practices

Balboa Press books may be ordered through booksellers or by contacting:

Balboa Press
A Division of Hay House
1663 Liberty Drive
Bloomington, IN 47403
www.balboapress.com
1 (877) 407-4847

Interior Image Credit: Melinda Parkhurst

ISBN: 978-1-9822-4679-2 (sc)
ISBN: 978-1-9822-4680-8 (e)

Print information available on the last page.

Balboa Press rev. date: 05/20/2020

BALBOA.PRESS
A DIVISION OF HAY HOUSE

This book is dedicated to my husband, Will, for supporting me in everything that I do; to my dear friends Janella, for being the inspiration behind the idea for this book, and Farai, for helping me stay on track, and my mentors and classmates at Atlantic University for broadening my world view in ways that I never could have imagined.

Table of Contents

Module 1 – The Journey Begins

"In life, finding a voice is speaking and living the truth. Each of you is an original. Each of you has a distinctive voice. When you find it, your story will be told. You will be heard." ~ John Grisham

As you have found your way to this book, you have probably been pondering, "Who am I?" The question is not a superficial one, but the search for who you are at the very core—your authentic self. This musing can prompt embarking on a journey of self-discovery to find meaning and purposeful connections in your daily life. To get to the heart of this requires challenging the thinking of, "This is just the way I am," and digging deep to discover why. This entails building awareness of your personality traits, habits, and intuitive abilities so you can leverage the strengths they offer and determine what to change or leave behind. Assessing your strengths and weaknesses, and the benefits embedded within them will help you build an abundant toolkit with which to navigate and cultivate a meaningful life.

Rumi said, "Our true self is rooted in love, awareness and creativity." To this end, this workbook is an invitation to embark upon a holistic journey exploring a variety of activities. You will engage in storytelling through journal prompts. Building mindfulness and movement practices will allow you to drop out of your thinking mind into a sense of flow, enabling you to transcend the everyday. You will also cultivate a connection with your intuition. Creative exercises will offer an opportunity not only to bring a sense of playfulness but also provide insight by providing a different perspective. You will foster a sense of empowerment that comes from knowing one's true self. Engagement in these activities brings awareness to the potential for transformation by recognizing a sense of self that encompasses a connection with others and to something greater than yourself. Stepping into the deeply personal connects us to the universal and opens a world of possibilities.

How to Use This Workbook

In the process of working through the activities in this book, you will be capturing your work and insights in a journal. You will be creating what is known as a visual or art journal because it will contain not only the written word but also the results of various creative exercises. These exercises are suitable for those with all levels of art experience, from those who can't remember the last time they used a colored pencil to someone who has a consistent practice. Engaging in creative endeavors such as art, movement, or writing can provide an avenue for intuition to flow. This can prompt insights into questions or problems, which are not evident with our usual modes of linear and logical thinking. Be open to explore the various mindfulness, movement, and creative exercises without expectation for the quality of the outcome. You never need to share your journal or the mindfulness and movement practices and creative processes that went into making it, so commit to the process with abandon. Consider the time you set aside for yourself and this process as sacred as it can inspire innovation in perspective and lead to personal growth and transformation. There is no right or wrong way to do any of these activities. Relax into the experience and embrace what comes.

Although some of the exercises require input from the previous ones, many of the individual sections can be completed as stand-alone activities. I invite you to work through the book in whatever manner feels intuitively right for you. If an exercise or practice doesn't resonate with you at the moment, skip it for now. You can always come back to it at a later time. This is your journey, so you are free to design it to suit you.

Gathering Supplies

You will need a few supplies for the creative exercises throughout this workbook.

- Journal – a lined, unlined, or bullet journal will work depending on your preference. My favorite is a generic sketchbook or journal with pages made for watercolor or mixed media. This type of paper won't wrinkle if you decide to use paints or any other material that is very wet. However, you can use whatever you like or have on hand—even a lined spiral notebook will work.
- Markers, colored pencils, pens and/or crayons
- Paint (watercolor or acrylic) or pastels (optional)
- Glue - sticks or liquid
- Scissors
- Old magazines, books, or catalogs for cutting up
- Washi tape – patterned masking tape (optional)
- Ephemera – scrap papers or memorabilia like ticket stubs, menus, lace, fabric, ribbon, stickers or anything else that might like to incorporate into a collage (optional)

This is the time to experiment with the art materials you have never used or the glittery gel pens you picked up at the drug store. Keep in mind that you don't need expensive supplies. For our purposes, the ones from the dollar store work just as well as those from the artist supply store, but feel free to try something new. I had the pleasure of meeting an artist who started using discarded makeup when she couldn't afford to buy art supplies. Find her inspiring story at http://gloriasart.com/meetgloria/.

Getting Grounded

We spend much of our everyday life moving from one distraction to the next. The world and pace of life seems to be in a constant swirl. To be able to begin the work of self-discovery, dropping out of the chaos is necessary. We will be using a grounding exercise to carve out a sacred space of calm for doing this work. Grounding is a process that allows you to reconnect to your body and the rhythms of the natural world. One of the easiest ways to do this is to focus on the breath.

Read through this guided meditation beforehand, and you will be able to follow through on your own without needing to refer to the text.

Into the Stillness

Sit comfortably and either lower your eyelids or close them, if that feels comfortable for you. Begin to focus on your breathing. Without trying to change anything, just observe the qualities of your breathing. Notice if it is shallow or deep, fast or slow. Notice if your breath is high in the chest or deep into the belly. Become aware of the rise and fall of your chest and the movement of your ribcage with each breath. For the next breath, breathe in for a count of 4 and exhale for a count of 6. Repeat this for 3 or 4 more times. Let your breath return to its normal pattern. When you are ready, open your eyes.

The Journey Begins

As you embark upon this journey, I hope that you enjoy the process of discovering aspects of your authentic self. It is empowering to build awareness of the tools that you have within you to call upon to navigate this complicated world. Also, taking time out to engage in a variety of mindfulness, movement, and creative activities supports your mental and physical wellbeing. I hope your experiences in revealing the stories of yourself leads you to find a sense of wholeness and opens a new world of possibilities for you.

Art **EMPOWERMENT** Toolkit Vision
Connection Stillness **MEANINGFUL** Path
Creativity Movement **Awareness**
Mindfulness INTUITION Stories Heart
Consciousness GRATITUDE Journey Purpose
CONFIDENCE **Authenticity Self** Love
Change STRENGTH Soul Growth **Journal**

Resources for Further Exploration

Big Magic, Elizabeth Gilbert
Creative Wildfire, L.K. Ludwig
Gloria's Art, http://gloriasart.com/meetgloria/
Visual Journaling, Barbara Ganim & Susan Fox

Module 2 – Legacy of Your Ancestors

"…one of the most priceless things we have — where we came from and how we got to be where we are." ~Alex Haley

There is a rich infrastructure that informs how you live your life that comes from both within and from the collective origins of your ancestors. Your parents and grandparents (and any other caretakers) drew conclusions about the world around them and built perceptions about themselves as they went about doing what was necessary to survive and develop in their daily lives. These beliefs may not have been verbalized and may have been imprinted so many generations ago, their origins are lost. Your ancestors consciously and unconsciously passed these generational values, beliefs, hopes, and dreams on to you, and it is for you to embrace, change, or release them. As you look back over your past, do so in a manner that feels right for you, knowing that you can always return to the present at any time. I invite you to explore and shine light on the path that led you to this moment. These explorations can bring up discomforting memories of pain or struggle. If you find yourself overwhelmed, please seek guidance from a close friend, family member, or a mental health professional.

Perspectives of Generations Past

To help gain perspective on their lives, ponder any memories or stories that you may have of your parents, their parents, and any other relatives or parental figures. Looking through old photos may also spark some memories. The following meditation will help establish an empathetic connection to them to gather a sense of how they managed to thrive as they met the challenges that they faced even if you do not have factual knowledge of these events.

Read through this guided meditation beforehand, then you will be able to follow through on your own without needing to refer to the text. Have your journal and pen handy to be ready for the journaling exercise that follows.

Into the Stillness

In a quiet place, make yourself comfortable and close or lower your eyelids if that feels right for you. Take several slow, deep breaths. Return to your regular breathing. Let go of any tenseness in the body.

Bring to mind a biological or adoptive parent, grandparent, or some other parental figure. Imagine yourself stepping into their shoes to experience things as they did. Take in the sights, sounds, and smells. Invite your intuition and imagination to get a sense of this person's perceptions of life, self, and the situation at that time with its advantages and limitations even though you may not have any precise knowledge of these events. What comes to you will flow from the connection to the heritage of your ancestors.

When you are ready, take a few deep cleansing breaths to return to the present. If you would like, offer a moment of gratitude for what your ancestor has passed on to you. Gently bring some movement to your body and open your eyes.

Journal Prompts

In your journal, write from the perspective of your relative to capture anything that came to you during your meditation. Let this flow from you without worrying about spelling, punctuation, or complete sentences. In your writing, you may find answers to some of these questions:

- What were some of your sources of joy and dissatisfaction?
- How did you understand your position within society, and what were its limitations, privileges, and responsibilities?
- Were you able to achieve your dreams?
- What hopes do you have for the future for yourself or your family?

Now from your view, reflect on how your intuitive connection to your ancestor's perspective is woven into your own. Perhaps this exercise will provide some insights into why you behave a certain way or look at life through a particular lens. This awareness offers the opportunity to evaluate if this perspective is a strength to be cultivated or released if it does not support who you are today.

Repeat this for any other of your relatives whose story you would like to explore further.

Creativity: Expressions of the Past

Look through old photographs that you may have of your childhood, family members, or their lives. Gather any ephemera such as ticket stubs, old letters, buttons, pictures from old magazines, etc. If there are any personal photos or papers that you particularly like, make copies of them so you can include them in your collage without damaging the original. You can use pictures clipped from magazines instead if you don't have photos or access to make copies. Using whatever art supplies you have on hand, create a page in your journal incorporating photos, drawings, ephemera, or words that tell some of the story of your ancestors.

Journal Prompts

Place your completed collage in a spot where you can see it. After a few moments of taking it in, write a journal entry to capture the wisdom offered by your artwork.

In this example, I used a copy of a photo of my paternal grandmother and great-grandmother and incorporated bits of antique lace and buttons, old papers, paints, and modeling paste to build layers of texture. I felt this provided a representation of the story of overcoming hardships that seem to be reflected in their faces. A section of my journal writing from my great-grandmother's perspective follows:

Descended from slavery and through all the struggles of everyday life, look how far we have come! The road will not be easy, but I hope for my daughter that she will have a chance to reach for her dreams and get more from life than I could even begin to imagine.

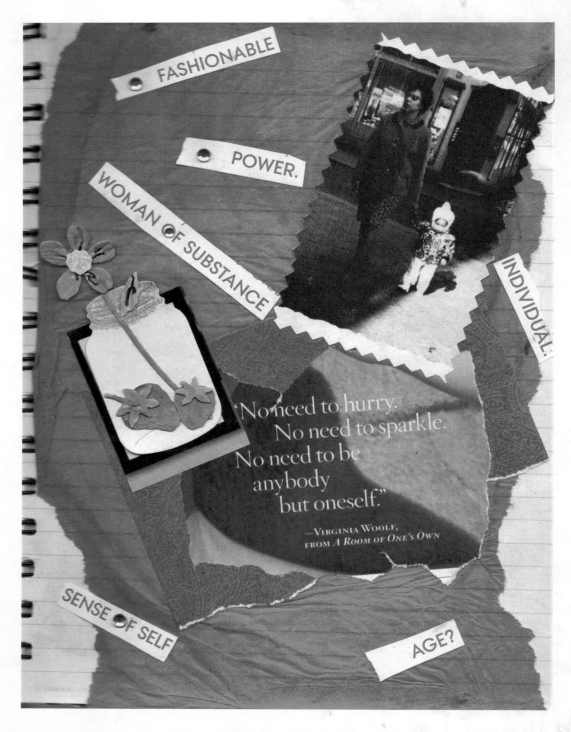

I used a copy of a photo of me holding my mother's hand as we ran errands. I incorporated some of the key messages from my journal writing based on stepping into my mother's perspective into this collage that uses scrap papers and words cut from old magazines.

Creating an Altar

Throughout my studies in yoga, dance, and meditation, I learned about various reasons people create altars. A common thread among those reasons is they offer you a place to gather items that are important to you and can serve as a reminder to take a moment to be present and grounded. I use a side table under my window in my study. It holds a few plants to connect me to nature along with a small bowl of crystals, stones, feathers, and shells collected on various adventures. Photos of my parents and me as a baby perch atop a rotating stack of books. There are mementos from friends and family, a candle and an incense burner. The space around this altar is where I will often sit to read or pause for a moment of reflection, contemplation, or gratitude. Consider creating an altar space and bringing into it things that have deep meaning for you and connect you to others, both past, and present, to a higher consciousness, or your spirituality. You may want to take a few moments at your altar to offer gratitude to your ancestors.

This is the low side table that I use for my altar. It is the right height for when I sit on the floor on a cushion.

A corkboard or shelf can make a good altar if floor space is limited.

Resources for further exploration

Perspectives of Generations Past
    The Four-Fold Way, Angeles Arrien, Ph.D
    Inner Excavation, Liz Lamoreaux
    Personal Mythology, David Feinstein, PhD and Stanley Krippner, PhD
    Journal to the Self: Twenty-two Paths to Personal Growth, Kathleen Adams
Creating an Altar
    Inner Excavation, Liz Lamoreaux

Module 3 – Our Many Masks

"Your vision will become clear only when you can look into your own heart. Who looks outside, dreams; who looks inside, awakens." ~ Carl Jung

Your authentic self is how you truly feel when you are not distracted by the external environment. It is what makes you unique and underpins how you relate to the world. This often-unconscious higher state of our being connects us to the oneness of life, provides a quality of continuity, and sparks our sensitivity and creativity. It is frequently in the background as we experience daily living.

On the other hand, our personality is how we appear to others and is based on the image that we project into the world. This façade can sometimes be different than our authentic self and consists of mannerisms and our imitation of others. It is driven by habits and is characterized by predictable behavior. We create this veneer to protect our vulnerability as we negotiate how to fit into societal norms. To command a situation or complete a task, we can bring forward either authentic or conditioned personality traits. In any case, we navigate a multi-faceted array of roles that radiate from and are influenced by our authentic core. We will explore the many faces you present to the world and bring awareness to the effects of culture on how you navigate daily life. By using creative projects to depict these roles visually, there can be an illumination into those that are most valued and others that have become obsolete, and it is time to let them go.

Wheel of Personality

Our authentic core is surrounded by the various personas that we wear as we function in everyday life. Like the spokes of a wheel (or petals of a flower), these roles radiate out to be shared with the world. Here is an example:

Journal Prompts

Either use the wheel below or draw one into your journal and capture a facet of your personality for each of the sections. You may not need them all or add more if necessary.

14

Into the Stillness

Self-observation is standing aside and watching oneself go by. It requires an extraordinary type of attention that allows you to be aware of what you are doing as well as observing your thoughts and feelings without judgment. If these observations are made with loving-kindness and with objectivity, they will bring your unconscious behaviors into your awareness. This will allow you to reflect on your roles and how you approach them to ascertain if they are harmonious or in conflict with your true self.

For example, you will find yourself running late again to your book club meeting, and always seem to come away feeling grumpy and drained. During the discussion, you find that you aren't engaging in the banter and look forward to getting home to curl up on the couch with the new book you are reading. Engaging in self-observation during this event may reveal that you are no longer enjoying the book selections and the discussion seems to always turn to the latest episode of some show you don't watch. Upon further reflection, you realize that you go out of habit because you had more in common with the others when your children were younger, but your current interests have shifted. It may be time to let this activity go and keep in contact in other ways.

Capture your observations in your journal, and you will be better able to recognize any negative or obsolete habits. This process may be new for you, so you will not always remember to do it. It is a skill that develops over months and years. However, it will become easier the more often you do it, and the insights you gain will support you in your journey of growth and transformation.

The Influence of Culture

The society and culture in which you were raised have distinctive stamps on the way you think and do things. Prevailing customs often unconsciously characterize your activities and thinking, and these influences are often difficult to discern as you go about your everyday life. These presumptions affect everything from how you dress and present yourself, your role in relationships, and what activities and careers you pursue. Today, we are bombarded by external expectations from not only our families, communities, magazines, and television, but by the constant barrage of the internet and social media. Although a culture's accumulated wisdom helps bridge the past with the present by providing guidance, it often lags in adapting to fit an ever-changing environment. However, awareness of the effects these forces can have on you offers the opportunity for challenging the fit of the prevailing beliefs and culture with your evolving authentic self. As you mature and assimilate new experiences, you may discover that you are at odds with the dominant culture. You have the freedom to decide if you will dig deeper and broaden your self-knowledge, opening to the possibility for personal transformation. You have the power of choice as to what extent you will assimilate the changes inwardly or project them into the world around you.

Journal Prompts

In a journal entry, examine how who you are fits with cultural and societal expectations. Examine what would it be like for you if you did not have such expectations to consider and ponder if you would make any changes in your life. Capture any thoughts you have about how you have changed as you have matured.

Creativity: Seeing Me

Although we may often see our reflection in the mirror as we get dressed or take photos to share online, we infrequently take the time to look at ourselves honestly. For this project, you will be making a collage of images of yourself. Look through old photographs and make copies of any that you might like to use. Check through the shots that you did not share with others as they often show the real you. Another source of photos for this exercise is to take a few snapshots of yourself from perspectives you wouldn't usually use for public pictures. You can prop your camera on the ground or use a tripod or a high shelf to shoot from overhead. Experiment getting up close or being at a distance. Capture your reflection in a mirror or take a snap of your feet where you stand. This is an opportunity to let down your guard and have fun. You don't have to share these with anyone else, so pick the ones that feel intuitively representative of who you are at your core. Gather any ephemera such as ticket stubs, old letters, buttons, pictures from old magazines, etc., and use whatever art supplies you have on hand to create a page in your art journal that captures who you are in the present moment.

This collage contains copies of photos, newsprint, washi tape, stamps, and markers on a background of pastels and acrylic paint.

Movement Exercise

Place your completed collage in a spot where you can see it. If it feels right, put on your favorite music, or revel in the silence, then move in any way that feels good to you from some simple swaying to full out dancing with fist pumps, spins, and air guitar. Let your collage inspire your movements. After a song or two (or 5-10 minutes of quiet) settle down in a comfortable position with your collage and journal nearby. Take a few moments to place your awareness on your breath as it returns to normal. Become aware of the sensations in your body after your movement exercise: notice your ribs expand with your breath, notice the muscles in your legs and arms, and take in how you feel. When you are ready, complete the journal exercise that follows.

Journal Prompts

Create a journal entry to capture the wisdom offered by your artwork and how that translated into the flow of movement through your body. Your words may come to you as poetry, a song lyric, or a story—however, they come to you is right for this moment. If you need some help getting the words flowing, start with I am… statements. For example:

I am bold and will not stand silent when I have something to say.
I am adventurous but not reckless.
I am forging ahead even when I am uncertain of all the details.
I am not a late bloomer but shine when the time is right.
I am learning to appreciate the journey as much as the destination.

I decided to incorporate my statements into my collage, as shown above.

Resources for further exploration

Wheel of Personality

Soul-Purpose, Mark Thurston

Breaking the Habit of Being Yourself, Dr. Joe Dispenza

Influence of Culture

Inner Excavation, Liz Lamoreaux

Living on Purpose, Dan Millman

Creativity: Seeing Me

Inner Excavation, Liz Lamoreaux

Living into Art, Lindsay Whiting

Module 4 – Your Personal Timeline

"We do not see things as they are, we see them as we are."~ Anaïs Nin

No matter whether you think about it or not, your past invariably weaves its way into your present. The threads of your ancestors, other personally influential people, and your own life experiences make up the tapestry of who you are today. As you experience personal growth and maturity, your perspectives and understanding of meaning shifts, so taking time to review key events and moments can offer insights that you were not able to access previously. Key moments are markers in your life that gave you pause to feel that you would never be the same again, or when you felt particularly connected to others or something greater than yourself. These extraordinary moments are also known as peak experiences. As you contemplate these pivotal events that make up your personal timeline, keep in mind that they are neutral and invite an openness to explore the gifts of wisdom they have to offer. Peak experiences can be of times of achievement, but also of sorrow or struggle. If you find yourself overwhelmed, please seek guidance from a close friend, family member, or a mental health professional

Building Your Timeline

You will be creating a list of 10-15 significant moments in your life. You can build your collection of milestones from a variety of perspectives. They may come to you chronologically or randomly. After you have collected your list, you can then put them in chronological order to see any patterns or rhythms. No matter how many times you do this exercise, you will likely have a slightly different list each time. As your life circumstances shift, the events that affect you change. Trust your intuition will bring the markers that are right for this time in your life. No matter which of the perspectives you choose to construct your list, the first item should be, "I was born." The following are examples of some of the themes around which to build your list:

General

1. I was born in California
2. We moved to Germany
3. We moved to Texas
4. We moved to Pennsylvania
5. We moved to Texas
6. My brother was born.
7. We moved to Taiwan
8. We moved to Texas
9. I got married.
10. My son was born.
11. I moved to Ohio
12. I moved to Delaware
13. I got divorced.
14. I got married.
15. I moved to the Washington, DC metro area

Body

1. I was born.
2. I learned to swim.
3. I took ballet classes.
4. I won 3rd place in a youth tennis tournament.
5. I was on the high school drill team.
6. I was in gymnastics.
7. I competed in dance competitions.
8. I had a baby.
9. I performed semi-professionally as a dancer.

Feeling

1. I was born.
2. I felt cared for and loved.
3. I felt insecure and lost.
4. I felt happy and confident.
5. I felt overwhelmed.
6. I felt confident.
7. I felt stifled.
8. I felt confident and secure.
9. I felt sadness and grief.
10. I felt open

Peak experiences (Intuitive)

1. I was born.
2. I had distinct moments of awareness at the age of three.
3. I connected strongly to dogs.
4. I connected strongly to being in nature.
5. I practiced mind reading with a junior high school friend.
6. I practiced yoga with my mother.
7. I ignored my intuition but learned to trust it in the future.
8. I worked with a team on several complex projects that went exceptionally well. I trusted my intuition to make a significant change in my life.
9. My spouse and I can sometimes read each other's thoughts.
10. I am in a group of dancers whose collaborations are a joy to create and share.
11. I begin studying and practicing meditation.
12. I listened to my intuition to find the continuing education programs that will prepare me for the next phase in my life.
13. I had several messages in my dreams from my mother after her passing.

Read through the following guided meditation beforehand, and you will be able to follow through on your own without needing to refer back to the text. Have your journal and pen handy to be ready for the journaling exercise that follows.

Into the Stillness

In a quiet place, make yourself comfortable and close or lower your eyelids if that feels right for you. Take a slow, deep breath in and exhale it completely. Repeat two or three times. Notice any tension you may be holding in your forehead, neck, shoulders, and hands and breathe into it until the tension releases. Soften your eyes and relax your jaw.

Imagine that you are in a theater. This is a safe space. Playing on the screen are the images of your life. Without becoming engaged in the stories, watch as the important moments of your life unfold from birth until the present day. The only thing you need to do is notice and feel. Stay and watch for as long as you like. When you are ready, take a deep cleansing breath or two, then open your eyes.

Journal Prompts

In your journal, create your list of 10-15 key moments for your timeline. You can use single words or short phrases, but capture the thoughts as they flow. Once you have completed your list, you can organize it in chronological order if it did not come to you in that form. After completing your timeline, you may want to take some time to capture any feelings, observations, or insights about any of the moments in your journal.

Creativity: Key Moments Mandala

For this project in your art journal, you will be creating a mandala that will symbolize some of the key moments from your timeline. Mandala is the Sanskrit word for a sacred circle. Mandalas are a primal circular pattern that can be found throughout nature in webs, snowflakes, flowers, our eyes, crystals, an atom, our cells, and so much more. When we work with mandalas, we are connecting to this universal pattern that is within and all around us. Everything radiates from the still point at the center. Mandalas represent wholeness, and working with them can offer a sense of inner peace by bringing order to the chaos. Mandalas are representative of the circle of life, and you will explore your timeline in this circular form in the creation of a mandala.

Gather any of the art supplies you would like to use, your timeline list, and your journal. On a blank page, draw a large circle. If you don't have a compass, you can draw around the edge of a plate. Then divide your circle into four wedges — one for each: childhood, young adulthood, adulthood, and the present.

Look at your timeline list to see which entries fit into the time of your youth. Now take a moment to reflect on this with your eyes closed if that is comfortable for you. What would it be like if you could represent how that time was for you as an image or symbol? Open your eyes and draw or paint what came to you into one of the wedges in your mandala. When you have completed that section, repeat this process for each of the other sections for young adulthood, adulthood, and the present.

The following are examples of mandalas created from timeline lists of different perspectives.

Starting in the upper right, the section for childhood contains bright sunshine, a simple flower, and a clear sky which represent newness, beauty, and simplicity to me. The next section for young adulthood, offers different patterns and colors of all the varied experiences, people and worldviews that I was exposed to with a winding path that offers a fork indicating a life-altering choice I had to make. The section of adulthood shows the chaos and difficult choices I had to make followed by an untangling of confusion and finally a calm as I settled into who I was becoming. The final section contains a building that represents stability, a clear night sky with twinkling stars that represent clarity, and an open lighted doorway suggesting welcoming and opportunities should I decide to step through.

This mandala depicts my timeline from the perspective of the physical (appreciating both the strengths and gracefulness of my physical form), emotional (maturity allowing the blossoming of awareness), mental (mindfulness practices allowing me to be more mentally focused and alert) and spiritual (connecting to nature and the vastness of the universal unconsciousness)

Journal Prompts

Once you have completed your mandala. Take a few moments to take it in, then capture any insights you gain into your journal. Some prompts to consider:

- Do you notice any common threads that run through the symbols you have chosen?
- Do any of the symbols you chose have alternate meanings?
- Describe your feelings from those periods.
- Did this reflection bring forward any other key moments that you had forgotten?

Resources for Further Exploration

Building Your Timeline

Journal to the Self: Twenty-two Paths to Personal Growth, Kathleen Adams

Key Moments Mandala

Creative Wisdom: Mandala Introduction, Kathleen Horne

Module 5 – Strengths, Talents, and Connecting to the Higher Self

"Take full account of the excellencies which you possess, and in gratitude remember how you would hanker after them, if you had them not." ~Marcus Aurelius

You have an array of strengths and skills that you can call upon to create a fulfilling life. Some of these talents emerged naturally, while others developed through the nurture of training and practice. It may be difficult to think of yourself as a talented person because we tend towards a comparison of ourselves to others. However, the goal is not to evaluate to what degree you possess an aptitude but to know that it is available for you to call upon as you navigate the world. Talents are not always obvious but may be hidden. Some may have been put aside and forgotten to make way for the obligations of every living or because you were discouraged or teased for your early attempts. It may now be time to bring those hidden talents forward.

Although we can easily recognize them in others, we can have difficulty in identifying our own strengths and talents. By exploring both conscious thinking and intuition, you will build awareness of the wealth of talents that you possess. To help overcome the blinders that may be blocking your view, the following exercises will provide creative options to discover the abilities you have within you.

Creativity: Exploring Strengths and Talents

Sometimes facing a blank page can be overwhelming and stifle the flow of thoughts. An alternate method to create a list of your strengths and talents is to create a mind map. A mind map is a relationship diagram that shows the connections between pieces of information in a non-linear manner. They provide a way of building awareness of how diverse information relates to the whole.

On a blank page in your journal, draw a circle in the middle and write the main topic to be explored in the center. In this case, My Strengths and Talents.

Then take a word or phrase that comes to mind and write it a short distance away and connect it with a line to the center. Next, see what idea the new word evokes and write it near the first word and connect those two words with another line.

movement ——— yoga
choreography
Teaching
performances
Dancer

bringing people together
events
motivating others
coordinating effort
leading
mentoring

My Strengths + Talents

organizational skills
create admin processes
Implement
training

Keep doing this process until you run out of connecting ideas. Then go back to the center and choose another thought and repeat this process until you run out of ideas. The idea is that one thought triggers another, which then triggers the next idea. As you are going through this process, don't worry about how or why the thoughts are connected, just capture them in whatever order they appear. There is no one way to draw your map, so write it as it comes.

You will end up with something that may look like this.

A mind map is not meant to be orderly or neat, but allow you to capture the process of your thinking. Reflection will allow you to uncover insights and connections between them.

Journal Prompts

Place your mind map where you can see it. Create a journal entry to capture the wisdom it offers. Make a list of the strengths and talents from your mind map. Some may be quite clear, but others may require you to think a bit about what they mean to you. As you review the diagram, you may find that this inspires new words. Also, look for replication of the same or similar words across your many branches as they provide clues to specialized skills that you possess. To help with this task, I annotated replicated words with the same color symbols to aid in making my list. As shown in the following example, I grouped training, teaching, and mentoring together.

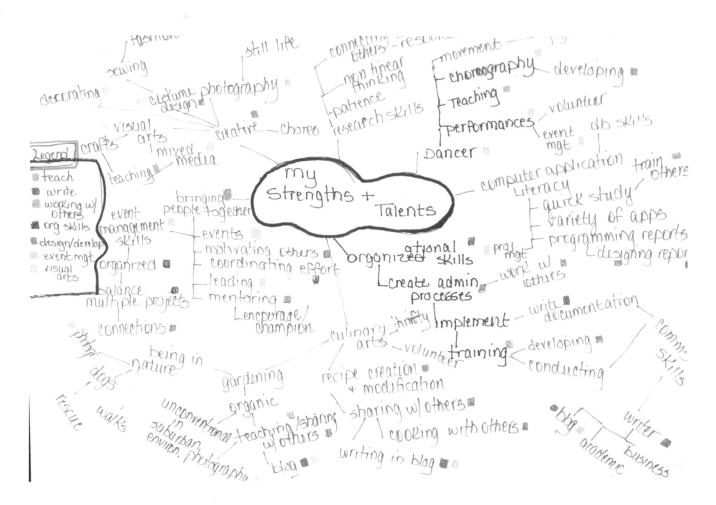

Uncovering Your Hidden Strengths

There are skills that we intuitively know we have or have been put aside from our youth. Now may be the time to bring these hidden abilities forward for the journey ahead. Try the following exercise to help bring these dormant talents into your conscious mind.

Peak Experiences

Peak experiences are moments when you felt connected to something outside of or greater than yourself. You may have been aware of intuitive sensitivity where you were able to know the right choices without going through all of the mental processing to arrive at a decision. These can also be times where you have experienced heightened creativity, activity, or performance, and everything seemed to flow effortlessly. You may have lost track of time and space as you were completely absorbed in the activity.

Journal Prompts

In your journal, capture any peak moments that you recollect from childhood to present. These moments can happen not only in extraordinary times but also in the most ordinary of circumstances. Consider experiences from your past that may include:

- A special time in nature
- A moment of deep love

- A time of flow in creativity
- An extraordinary moment of clarity

After you have captured these experiences, underline any words that represent the strengths or talents you possess.

Movement Exercise

You will be doing this practice outside, so bring your journal or a small notepad and pen with you. Find a place where you have some room to move around like your yard or a park. If possible, take off your shoes so you can feel grounded to the earth. Take a few deep cleansing breaths. Hold the intention in your mind of uncovering your hidden and forgotten strengths. Now, walk slowly forward. Open your hand and let one of your forgotten or hidden abilities fall into your hand from the sky. Name it. Do this 5-10 times. Write down what came to you in your journal. This may spark memories of other abilities that you can capture in your journal too.

Dreams

Dreams provide clues to what is going on in your waking life. You may already have a vibrant dream life, and if you consistently capture them in a journal, you will have a library of entries that can review to provide insight into your strengths and talents. However, if yours are like mine, your dreams may need a bit of coaxing to make themselves known. As has been documented as far back as to the dream temples of ancient Greece, it is possible to create a practice to incubate a dream. If you follow the steps in the following mindfulness exercise, you may find that you can experience better dream recall that will provide insights into questions you have had in mind.

Into the Stillness

To incubate a dream, it is important to set a sincere intention and be open to receive guidance. Have a journal or notepad and pen beside your bed to record your dream before it slips away. Pick a night when you think there is a good chance that you will sleep well and when you will have about 15 minutes in the morning to record your experience in your journal. If possible, pick a night when you do not have to be awakened by an alarm in the morning such as on a weekend. Abrupt awakening can cause the dream to disappear before you can record it.

During the evening that you incubate a dream, allow some time to write in your journal exactly what it is that you want to know. In this case, you are looking for guidance about your strengths and talents such as:

- What are my hidden strengths?
- What talents have I ignored?

As you prepare for bed, give yourself the suggestion to remember your dreams and hold your question in your mind as you settle down into sleep.

Whenever you awaken and before you get out of bed, write down any dreams that you recall or thoughts that come immediately to mind even if they do not seem relevant to your question. Even if you do not specifically recall a dream, the thoughts that appear on awakening have the potential to provide clues for you.

Journal Prompts

Examine your dream notes. Look for any apparent skills you and others are using that you recognize from your dreams. You may also find that you are applying expertise that you do not currently use in your waking life. Capture any thoughts or feelings evoked by your dreams as they are the messages from your intuition. If you are stymied in finding meaning in a dream, you may find inspiration for interpretation from http://www. dreammoods.com/. The suggestions there may not always feel the perfect fit but may spark inspiration for making sense of an unclear dream. However, whatever meaning seems intuitively right is the one to use, as your interpretation is the only one that matters.

Resources for Further Exploration

Creativity: Exploring Strengths and Talents

> *The Achievement Habit,* Bernard Roth

Uncovering Hidden Strengths

> *Life is a Verb,* Patti Digh

> *Living on Purpose,* Dan Millman

Peak Experiences

> *Soul-Purpose,* Mark Thurston

Dreams

> *Dream Moods* http://www.dreammoods.com/

> *Dream Solutions! Dream Realizations!,* Henry Reed

> *The Secret History of Dreaming,* Robert Moss

Module 6 – Discovering Strengths within Weaknesses and Amassing Your Toolkit of Talents

"For people to achieve all that is demanded of them, they must regard themselves as greater than they are." ~ Goethe

We each rely on a library of skills for navigating life's challenges without giving much thought to that process. With some time spent in contemplation, you can build a catalog of characteristics and skills that you can consciously call upon as needed. However, there is another source of talent that you may have overlooked—your faults and weaknesses. Our weaknesses are often strengths that have been misused or used to an extreme, which distorts them from being a beneficial asset to a hindrance. Excavating this untapped resource can equip you with additional tools. It may not surprise you that many people find it much easier to list their faults than their strengths and talents, and they do not spend much time considering how to extract the benefits from them. As much as we may prefer to avoid examining them, it is better to understand and learn from these weaknesses, as this can lead to opportunities for growth into your full potential.

Discovering the Strengths in Your Weaknesses

Journal Prompts

In your journal, create a list of 5 or 6 of your faults or weaknesses. For each one, look objectively to see if you can find the strengths that are within using the following prompts.

- Why am I doing this?
- Within this weakness, what strength is being exaggerated or distorted by stress or fear?

For example:

- Fault: Being bossy
- Why: Desire to create an exceptional product or outcome
- Strengths within: Leadership and organization skills, determination, attention to detail

Don't worry if you can't find the strengths in each of your faults. It can take time for the insights to come to you.

Another exercise that may provide insights into the talents hidden within your weaknesses is to take the list you created above and cross out any title you may have put across the top. Rename the list Assets for Growth. Reframing the list this way may give you another perspective in drawing out the beneficial aspects embedded within the weaknesses. Now, review the list and capture any additional strengths or talents that come to mind.

Into the Stillness

Examining your faults and weaknesses may have left you feeling a bit vulnerable or unsettled. One way to alleviate this feeling is to offer yourself a bit of compassion and foster a feeling of connectedness with others through the ancient practice of lovingkindness. This mindfulness practice directs the intention of the heart, first to ourselves, next to our loved ones, and then to extend outward to all sentient beings. Mahatma Gandhi said, "I believe in the essential unity of all beings, and so I understand deeply that if one person gains spiritually, the whole world gains." Therefore, offering loving thoughts and compassion inward towards yourself for the struggles and sorrows you face can allow you to find acceptance. This, in turn, can foster an openness that you can extend outward to both those close to you and to all other living beings to wish them to be filled with lovingkindness, peace, happiness, and healing.

Take a few moments to sit comfortably in a quiet place with your eyes lowered, or closed, to contemplate a sense of compassion for yourself, those you love, and all others. When you have completed this practice, take a few deep breaths to bring you back to the present moment before opening your eyes.

Most Admired Qualities

Journal Prompts

Take a moment to think about someone that you admire. It can be someone you know personally or a public figure from either the past or present. In your journal, describe all of the positive qualities that you admire about this person. Complete this task before reading on.

Now, look at this impressive list of qualities that you have captured. Would it surprise you that within you exist all of these qualities in some form as part of your authentic self? They may be fully formed traits or in development, or exist as potential that may, or may not, be realized in this lifetime. Through the concept of projection, we are attracted to the mirror of our inner selves in others. For example, if you admire the dedication someone has for helping children get access to good education, look to your own life to see how you mirror this behavior. Perhaps you collect books to donate to school libraries or work as a tutor.

This same technique also applies to the things about others that annoy you. If you are bothered when someone asks for help on their project assignments, reflect on your behavior to see if there may be something similar going on for you. If you maintain an openness to explore both the qualities you admire and those that you do not, there can be an opportunity for growth.

Building Your Toolkit of Strengths and Talents

Using the materials that you created from the previous exercises, you can now create a list of your strengths and talents. This set of tools will be available to support you as you navigate life. Although you will find that you focus on just a few at any given time, they are all available to call upon as necessary. This toolkit will expand as you have new experiences and continue the process of personal transformation.

Journal Prompts

Review any of the journal entries or art projects that you completed from any of the previous sections and write down all of the strengths and talents you find onto a fresh page in your journal. Look for the words and phrases that stand out for you. If your review inspires any new insight into hidden or forgotten talents, add these to the list as well.

When you have completed compiling your list, take a step back and look at what is likely quite a considerable list! Did you realize that you have such a well-stocked toolkit at your disposal? Add an entry in your journal detailing any revelations that the exercise of amassing your talents and strengths into a list has provided.

Movement Exercise

Indulge in a session of one of your favorite types of movement for 10-15 minutes. Walk or run a few blocks, do a few stretches, yoga poses, or tai chi, put on music and dance, pull weeds, chop wood, or engage in whatever movement feels good to you. Even just a few minutes of movement can clear your mind, re-energize your body, and bring fresh insights.

Creativity: Strengths and Talents

Having a visual representation of your toolkit of strengths and talents can inspire you when you find yourself stuck trying to find a solution to a problem. Seeing the tools that you have at your disposal in a glance may provide a shift that will bring a new perspective to the issue.

Gather your journal and art supplies. If you have some old magazines, you can clip or tear words and pictures that appeal to you. Create a page that is a visual representation of your strengths, talents, and skills that you can come back to when you feel a need for inspiration. The following are two examples of artwork representing a collection of strengths and talents.

This collage uses scrap papers, images torn out from magazines. The words are written with markers. The reclaimed envelope pocket contains little cards that each have a strength or talent written on it. The cards can be removed from the pocket and can be spread out when inspiration is needed.

This drawing uses pastels and markers to represent a collection of strengths and talents.

Journal Prompts

Place your strengths and talents artwork where you can see it. Take a few deep breaths to center yourself. Spend a few moments taking in your project. In your journal, capture any new insights, thoughts, or feelings that arise.

Resources for further exploration

Strengths and Weaknesses

> *The Art of Uncertainty,* Dennis Merrit Jones

> *Living on Purpose,* Dan Millman

> *Soul-Purpose,* Mark Thurston

Into the Stillness

> *Meditation for Beginners,* Jack Kornfield

Module 7 – Who Do You Want to Become?

"My mission in life is not merely to survive, but to thrive; and to do so with some passion, some compassion, some humor, and some style."– Maya Angelou

You may find that you are encountering conflict within and also between you and your external world. These areas of struggle are where your experiences have brought forth maturation to your authentic self. This growth may put you at odds with your beliefs and previous behavior patterns. This may also cause friction with those beliefs and behaviors of your family, friends, or society. Although this conflict can be unsettling, it is an invitation for inner exploration and the opportunity for growth and transformation. This is the time to discover and develop the stories of yourself and who you want to become.

Creativity: An Ideal Slice of Life

Gather your art supplies, including your journal, glue, scissors, and some old magazines that you can cut up. In preparation for making your collage, take a few moments to read through the following grounding mindfulness practice beforehand, then you will be able to follow through on your own without needing to refer to the text. You may want to try having some soft music ready to play while you work on your collage, or you may prefer to work in silence. If you decide to try some music, consider music from one of the following genres: jazz, classical, new age, nature, or meditation soundtracks—preferably something without lyrics to disrupt the connection to your inner guidance.

Into the Stillness

Sit comfortably and either lower your eyelids or close them, if that feels comfortable for you. Bring yourself into the present by taking a few deep breaths and releasing any tenseness you feel in your body especially in your brow, jaw, shoulders, hands, or toes. Now hold the intention of letting your inner guidance find what represents an ideal day or week for you. When you are ready, take 2 or 3 deep cleansing breaths and open your eyes.

Continue holding the intention of capturing how an ideal day or week looks for you. Turn on music if you have decided to use it. Take the old magazines and cut or rip out any photos or words that draw your attention. Make your choices without stopping to analyze why or what meaning might be associated with them.

Switching to your logical mind for this type of thinking will disrupt the connection of flow from your unconscious. After your collage is complete, you will reflect to find the messages being offered from within. For now, relax into the process. Allow yourself about 15-20 minutes to do this.

In a page in your journal, create a collage with some, or all, of the items you collected from the magazines. Feel free to add ephemera, paint, writing, or anything else that feels right to you.

This collage is made entirely from images and text cut from old magazines and represents activities and experiences I would like to have more often in my life.

Journal Prompts

Put your collage depicting your ideal slice of life where you can see it. Take some time to explore what you have captured here. In your journal, write about the details of your ideal day or week. Let the collage tell the story. Just let it flow without censoring your writing or thinking about whether your ideas are possible or how to make them happen. The following prompts may inspire some insights for you:

- Where are you?
- Who are the people around you?
- How are you spending your time?
- How do you feel?
- Is there anything that surprises you?

Assessing Conflicts Between Your Current Story and Your Ideal

Now that you have explored the possibilities for your ideal, it is time to contemplate the path that will head you in that direction of who you want to become. You may already realize that there are some conflicts between your current behavior and what is necessary to allow you to move towards the vision in your collage. This may require you to make some changes to how you have been doing things or with whom you spend your time. Additionally, identifying self-defeating behaviors, fears, and feelings of anxiety, dissatisfaction, or ambivalence will allow you to work with them and open the opportunity for healing. It will not always be easy because these changes may be in conflict with those who are close to you, your culture, and your own ingrained habits. However, developing awareness will bring these into your conscious thought, enabling you to make informed and intuitive choices.

Journal Prompts

Again, reflect on your ideal slice of life collage and your journal entry on your insights and wisdom from reflecting on your artwork. In a new journal entry, capture your thoughts about what obstacles you may need to overcome along your path to your ideal including:

- What behaviors or habits will you need to change to progress towards your ideal?
  Examples:
  - After work, I tend to watch television instead of working on my art.
  - I do not prioritize my own self-care on my list.
- What expectations do others have of you that must be negotiated?
  Example: Pursuing a career in the fashion industry is not acceptable in our family.
- Do you have any unrealistic fears to work through?
  Example: If I make these changes in my life, my friends will no longer be interested in spending time with me.
- Are there any activities that you will have to let go of to allow space for new ones?
  Example: Instead of surfing the internet shopping each evening, I will spend that time researching training programs.
- Are there any relationships that may need to shift in priority or be let go?
  Example: It would make me feel better to spend less time with the friend who always seems to be pessimistic about my endeavors.

Now that you have identified some of the changes you desire to make, it is time to take action.

Ritual of Release

Tear or cut a piece of paper into strips or squares. On each piece of paper, write down something that you are ready to let go of. You may find some inspiration in the previous section of assessing conflicts journal writing exercise, or there may be other habits or fears that you are ready to release. Fold or crumple each piece of paper. Choose one of the following methods:

- Burn the small pieces of paper in a fireplace or firepit.
- Put the pieces of paper in a small cardboard box or paper envelope and bury it.

As you prepare to either burn or bury your pieces of paper, hold them in your hands, and set your intention to release these no longer needed behaviors. With that, toss them into the flames or put them in a hole and cover them over.

Movement Exercise

As you watch your paper burn or as you cover up your box, indulge in whatever movement comes from the feeling of letting go. You may be inspired to chant, sing, clap, or be in stillness and silence. Whatever moves you is just right.

This ritual allows you to release pent-up energy, and consciously create space for something new to flow in. You will feel more empowered to be your authentic self when you give yourself permission to let go of what you no longer need.

Journal Prompts

In your journal, capture any new insights, thoughts, or feelings that arise after you have completed the ritual of release. Letting go of things that no longer have a place in who you are becoming may bring you a feeling of expansiveness. You may also feel a bit of apprehension as you let go of the familiar and begin to step into the unknown of new possibilities. Acknowledging all of these feelings through your journal and artwork provides an awareness that will help you be open to the opportunities that will come your way.

Resources for further exploration

An Ideal Slice of Life

A World of Artist Journal Pages, Dawn DeVries Sokol

Assessing Conflict between the current and the ideal

The 12 Secrets of Highly Creative Women, Gail McMeekin

Personal Mythology, David Feinstein, PhD and Stanley Krippner, PhD

Ritual of Release

The Art of Uncertainty, Dennis Merrit Jones

Module 8 – Bringing It All Together

"Trust yourself. Create the kind of self that you will be happy to live with all your life."~ Golda Meir

Although we have come to the end of this part of your journey, it is not truly the end—it is the beginning of consciously embodying your authentic self. You have done the work of exploring a good deal of what makes you who you are today. Your new experiences may cause other forgotten parts of your past to come to light. It is essential to take time for reflection and contemplation of how you want to assimilate those experiences and messages, and then, what actions you want to take in response. The stories of yourself will continue to evolve as your journey of personal growth and transformation becomes woven into the fabric of your being. You are the curator of how you want the expression of your authentic self to be conveyed.

Building an Ongoing Practice

I invite you to revisit any of these exercises and your journal entries when you feel discouraged or stuck. Reviewing your journal entries and artwork will remind you of where and how far you have come and the impressive toolkit of strengths and talents you have to draw upon. Choose one of the Into the Stillness mindfulness practices to ground you and connect you to your intuition. Engaging in a movement exercise can shift your focus from your thinking mind into a flow fostered by connecting to your body or being out in nature. This can stimulate connectivity to something greater than ourselves inviting openness and receptivity to possibilities previously blocked. These practices will also allow you to feel the shifts that are often so subtle you may miss them at first glance.

I would suggest that you set up a time for a periodic review to capture insights from your challenges and celebrate your progress. You will have updates to your toolkit of talents and perhaps some candidates for habits and obligations that you are ready to release. You can do these as often as you like. However, making this at least an annual practice tied to your birthday, the beginning of the new year, or some other specific date will make it a practice less likely to get forgotten in the busyness of everyday life. This is a holistic journey, so remember to find ways to nurture your body, mind, and spirit.

Into the Stillness

Sit comfortably and either lower your eyelids or close them, if that feels comfortable for you. Bring yourself into the present by taking a few deep breaths. Breathe in relaxation, breathe out tenseness. Breathe in ease, breathe out expectation. Hold the intention of acceptance and gratitude for all that you have experienced and openness for all that is yet to come. Bask in the stillness for as long as you would like. When you are ready, take 2 or 3 deep cleansing breaths and open your eyes.

Journal Prompts

In your journal, capture any insights, thoughts, or feelings that arise for you as you complete this inner exploration. Capture any visions you have for where you are heading next along your journey, projecting your authentic self into the world.

Gratitude

I would like to express gratitude for allowing me to share opportunities to explore avenues to unearthing your authentic self. The possibilities are limitless so may your inner wisdom lead you to discover a meaningful life. I hope you find that embodying the insights from the stories of who you are empowers you to know that you are enough.

Resources for further exploration

The Artist's Way, Julia Cameron

Something More: Excavating Your Authentic Self, Sarah Ban Breathnach

Bibliography

Adams, K. (1990). *Journal to the self: Twenty-two paths to personal growth.* New York, NY: Grand Central Publishing.

Arrien, A. (1992). *The Four-fold way: Walking the paths of the warrior, teacher, healer and visionary.* New York, NY: HarperOne.

Breathnach, S. B. (1998). *Something more: Excavating your authentic self.* New York, NY: Warner Books, Inc.

Cameron, J. (1992). *The artist's way: A spiritual path to higher creativity.* New York, NY: Jeremy P. Tarcher/Perigee.

Cunningham, L. B. (2010). *The mandala book: Patterns of the universe.* New York, NY: Sterling Publishing Co., Inc.

Digh, P. (2008). *Life is a verb: 37 days to wake up, be mindful, and live intentionally.* Guilford, CT: skirt! The Globe Pequot Press.

Dispenza, J. (2012). *Breaking the habit of being yourself: How to lose your mind and create a new one.* Carlsbad, CA: Hay House, Inc.

Dream Moods. Retrieved from: http://www.dreammoods.com/

Feinstein, D. and Krippner, S. (2008). *Personal mythology: Using ritual, dreams, and imagination to discover your inner story.* Santa Rosa, CA: Energy Psychology Press.

Ganim, B. and Fox, S. (1999). *Visual journaling: Going deeper than words.* Wheaton, IL: Quarry Books.

Gilbert, E. (2015). *Big magic: creative living beyond fear.* New York, NY: Riverhead Books.

Gloria's Art. Retrieved from: http://gloriasart.com/meetgloria/

Horne, Kathleen. (2019). *Creative wisdom: Mandala introduction.* Sarasota, FL: Expressive Arts Florida Institute.

Jones, D. M. (2011). *The art of uncertainty: How to live in the mystery of Life and Love It.* New York, NY: Jeremy P. Tarcher/Penguin.

Kornfield, J. (2008). *Meditation for beginners.* Boulder, CO: Sounds True, Inc.

Lamoreaux, L. (2010). *Inner excavation: Explore your self through photography, poetry and mixed media.* Cincinnati, OH: North Light Books.

Ludwig, L.K. (2010). *Creative wildfire: An introduction to art journaling—basics and beyond.* Beverly, MA: Quarry Books.

McMeekin, G. (2012). *The 12 secrets of highly creative women: A portable Mentor.* San Francisco, CA: Conari Press.

Millman, D. (2000). *Living on purpose: Straight answers to life's tough questions.* Novato, CA: New World Library.

Moss, R. (2009). *The secret history of dreaming.* Novato, CA: New World Library

Reed, H. (2007). *Dream solutions! Dream realizations! The original dream quest guidebook.* Mouth of Wilson, VA: Hermes Home Press

Roth, B. (2015). *The achievement habit: Stop wishing, start doing, and take command of your life.* New York, NY: HarperCollins Publishers.

Sokol, D. D. (2015). *A world of artist journal pages: 1000+ artworks - 230 Artists - 30 Countries.* New York, NY: Abrams.

Thurston, M. (1989). *Soul-purpose: Discovering and fulfilling your destiny.* New York, NY: St. Martin's Press.

Whiting, L. (2008). *Living into Art: Journeys through collage.* Boyes Hot Spring, CA: Paper Lantern

Photo credit: Jacci Duncan

About the author

Melinda Parkhurst revels in all things creative while being kind to the earth. She is an author of a creative lifestyle blog, tribal fusion dancer, avid gardener, mixed media artist, and photographer.

She has a B.S. in Information Systems and an M.A. in Transpersonal Psychology. She is a certified Vegan Lifestyle Coach and Educator (VLCE) and pursuing a Meditation Teacher Training certification. She is passionate about rescue dogs and volunteers with organizations that help eradicate hunger in the local community.

She believes that everyone who desires to find their authentic self, develop their creative voice, or live a more healthful lifestyle can do so even with limited resources. She is certain that it is never too late to start the journey—it takes letting go of expectations and enjoying the process.

MELINDAPARKHURST.COM

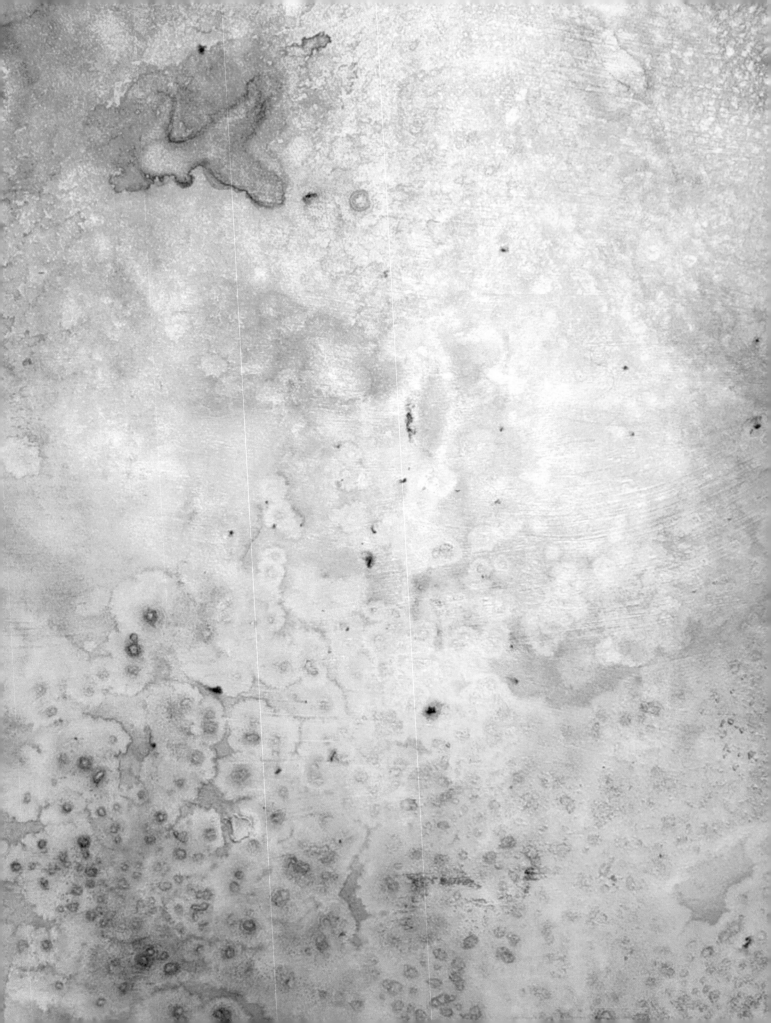

Printed in the United States
By Bookmasters